To

From

Let there be Peace

Panographs® by Ken Duncan

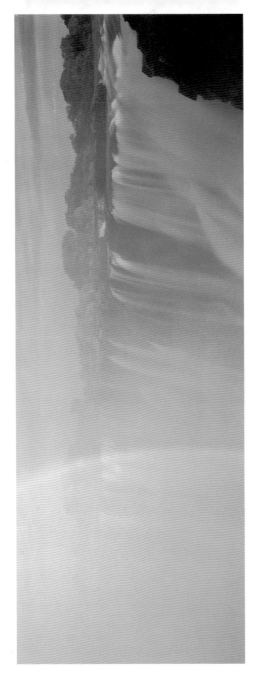

INTRODUCTION

As you gaze upon the beauty of God's creation in these photographs, may the inspired wisdom of the accompanying text lift your spirit to the knowledge of an awesome God. Our planet earth hurtles through space at 108,000 km per hour. At that speed you need a good driver and only God has the credentials. So, jump in the back seat and enjoy the ride, for true peace comes from knowing and trusting Him. This is the peace of God which transcends all understanding.

When peacemakers
plant seeds of peace,
they will harvest
justice.

Don't mistreat
someone who has
mistreated you.
But try to earn the
respect of others,

and do your best
to live at peace
with everyone.

Don't worry
about anything,

but pray
about everything.
With thankful hearts
offer up your prayers
and requests to God.

Then, because you belong to Christ Jesus, God will bless you with peace that no one can completely understand.

And this peace
will control the way
you think and feel.

When the Spirit
is given to us
from heaven,
deserts will become
orchards thick as
fertile forests.

Honesty and justice
will prosper there,
and justice will
produce lasting peace
and security.

You, the LORD's
people, will live
in peace, calm
and secure...

Jesus said,
"I give you peace,
the kind of peace
that only I can give.

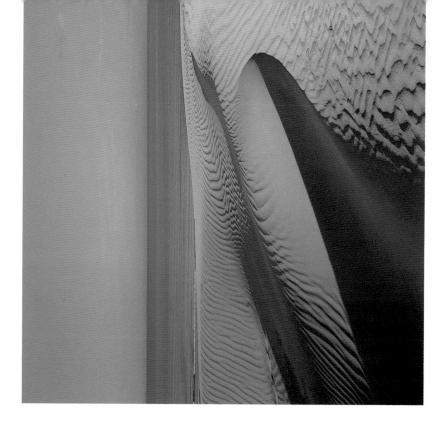

It isn't like
the peace that
this world can give.

So don't
be worried
or afraid."

I pray that
the LORD will bless
and protect you,

and that
he will show you
mercy and kindness.

May the LORD
be good to you and
give you peace.

When peacemakers plant seeds of peace,
they will harvest justice.

JAMES 3:18

Don't mistreat someone who has
mistreated you. But try to earn the
respect of others, and do your best to live
at peace with everyone.

ROMANS 12:17-18

Don't worry about anything, but pray
about everything. With thankful hearts
offer up your prayers and requests to
God. Then, because you belong to Christ
Jesus, God will bless you with peace that
no one can completely understand. And
this peace will control the way you think
and feel.

PHILIPPIANS 4:6-7

When the Spirit is given to us from
heaven, deserts will become orchards
thick as fertile forests.
Honesty and justice will prosper there,
and justice will produce lasting peace
and security.
You, the LORD's people, will live in peace,
calm and secure.

ISAIAH 32:15-18

Jesus said, "I give you peace, the kind of
peace that only I can give. It isn't like
the peace that this world can give. So
don't be worried or afraid."

JOHN 14:27

I pray that the LORD will bless and protect
you, and that he will show you mercy
and kindness.
May the LORD be good to you and give
you peace.

NUMBERS 6:24-26

PHOTO INDEX

Front cover: Davistown Jetty,
New South Wales, Australia

Page 2:   Victoria Falls, Zimbabwe, Africa

Page 4-5:   Sunflower sunrise, Gunnedah,
New South Wales, Australia

Page 6-7:   Quarry Beach, Mallacoota,
Victoria, Australia

Page 8-9:   Strzelecki Ranges, Victoria,
Australia

Page 10-11:   Oak Creek, Arizona, USA

Page 12-13:   Natural Arch, Queensland,
Australia

Page 14-15:   Terrigal Beach, New South Wales,
Australia

Page 16-17:   Grand Canyon, Arizona, USA

Page 18-19:   Somersby Falls, Central Coast,
New South Wales, Australia

Page 20-21:   Cape Leveque, Western Australia

Page 22-23:   Fan palms, Cape Tribulation,
Queensland, Australia

Page 24-25:   Uluru, Northern Territory, Australia

Page 26-27:   Refuge Cove, Victoria, Australia

Page 28-29:   Dove Lake, Cradle Mountain,
Tasmania, Australia

Page 30-31:   Dividing Line, Kambalda,
Western Australia

Page 32-33:   Gunyah Beach, Coffin Bay,
South Australia

Page 34-35:   The Twelve Apostles, Victoria,
Australia

Page 36-37:   Farmland near the Glass House
Mountains, Queensland, Australia

Page 38-39:   Norah Head Lighthouse,
New South Wales, Australia

Page 40-41:   Millstream Falls, Queensland,
Australia

Page 42-43:   Walls of Jerusalem National Park,
Tasmania, Australia

Page 44-45:   Whitsunday Island,
Queensland, Australia

Let there be Peace

Let there be Peace
First published in 1997
Reprinted 1999, 2002, 2003, 2004
by Ken Duncan Panographs® Pty Ltd
ABN 21 050 235 606
PO Box 3015, Wamberal NSW 2260
Telephone: +61 2 4367 6777
Email: panos@kenduncan.com

The National Library of Australia
Cataloguing-in-Publication entry:
Duncan, Ken.
Let there be Peace
Includes index
ISBN 0 9586681 4 0
1. Photographs - Collections. 2. Peace of
mind. I. Title
779.3

Photography© Ken Duncan 1997
CEV Text© American Bible Society 1995
Printed and bound in China
To view the range of Ken Duncan's
panoramic Limited Edition Prints
visit our Galleries situated at:
• 5740 Oak Road, Matcham, NSW
Telephone +61 2 4367 6701

• 73 George Street,
The Rocks, Sydney, NSW
Telephone +61 2 9241 3460
• Shop U6 Southgate,
Melbourne, VIC
Telephone +61 3 9686 8022
• Shop 14, Hunter Valley Gardens Village,
Broke Road, Pokolbin, NSW
Telephone +61 2 4998 6711

VISIT THE KEN DUNCAN GALLERY ON LINE: www.kenduncan.com